United States
Department of
Agriculture

Forest Service

Southern
Research Station

Resource Bulletin
SRS–173

Tennessee's Timber Industry—An Assessment of Timber Product Output and Use, 2009

James W. Bentley,
Tony G. Johnson,
and Doug Schnabel

I0450375

The Authors:

James W. Bentley, Forester, U.S. Forest Service, Southern Research
Station, Knoxville, TN 37919; **Tony G. Johnson**, Forester, U.S.
Forest Service, Southern Research Station, Asheville, NC 28804; and
Doug Schnabel, Forest Business Specialist, Tennessee Department of
Agriculture, Division of Forestry, Nashville, TN 37204.

May 2011

Southern Research Station
200 W.T. Weaver Blvd.
Asheville, NC 28804

Foreword

This report contains the findings of a 2009 canvass of all primary wood-using plants in Tennessee, and presents changes in product output and residue use since 2007. It complements the Forest Inventory and Analysis annual inventory of volume and removals from the State's timberland. The canvass was conducted to determine the amount and source of wood receipts and annual timber product drain, by county, in 2009 and to determine interstate and cross-regional movement of industrial roundwood. Only primary wood-using mills were canvassed. Primary mills are those that process roundwood in log or bolt form or as chipped roundwood. Examples of industrial roundwood products are saw logs, pulpwood, veneer logs, poles, and logs used for composite board products. Mills producing products from residues generated at primary and secondary processors were not canvassed. Trees chipped in the woods were included in the estimate of timber drain only if they were delivered to a primary domestic manufacturer.

A 100-percent canvass of all wood processors in Tennessee was conducted in 2010 to obtain information for 2009. In addition, roundwood from out-of-State mills known to be using logs or bolts harvested from Tennessee timberland was incorporated into Tennessee production estimates. Each mill was canvassed by mail or through personal contact at plant locations. Telephone contacts followed mailed questionnaire responses when additional information or clarification of a response was necessary. In the event of a nonresponse, data collected in previous surveys were updated using current data collected for mills of similar size, product type, and location. Surveys for all timber products other than pulpwood began in 1949, and are currently conducted every 2 years.

Pulpwood production data were taken from an annual canvass of all southern pulpmills. Medium density fiberboard, insulating board, and hardboard plants were included in this survey.

Acknowledgments

The Southern Research Station (SRS) gratefully recognizes the tremendous effort provided by the Tennessee Department of Agriculture, Division of Forestry staffs in the task of collecting the mill and facility information and Debra Dawson in processing and checking all the data. Appreciation and gratitude is extended to the forest industry and mill owners for providing their timber products information.

The authors thank David Arnold and Dave Walters for review and comments; Carolyn Steppleton and Michael Howell for their tireless efforts in processing and accuracy of the data; Helen Beresford for timber product output database maintenance and support; Anne Jenkins, Janet Griffin, Sharon Johnson, and Charlene Walker for tables, graphs, statistical checking, and styling; and the SRS Technical Publications Team for editorial review and publication of this report.

Timber Product Output Database Retrieval System

The Forest Inventory and Analysis (FIA) Research Work Unit of the USDA Forest Service developed the Timber Product Output (TPO) Database Retrieval System to help customers answer questions about timber harvesting and use in the Southern Region. This system acts as an interface to a standard set of consistently coded TPO data for each State and county in the region and Nation. This regional and national set of TPO data consists of 11 variables that describe for each county the roundwood products harvested, logging residues left in the woods, other timber removals (i.e. land clearing and reserved timber removals), and wood and bark residues generated by the county's primary wood-using mills. The system is available through the FIA Web site: http://srsfia2.fs.fed.us/.

The database is well documented and easy to use. The retrieval system allows the user to select the TPO variables of interest and generate a standard set of timber products, removals, and mill residue tables for the specified resource area, State, or region. The system has been logically divided into two sections to assist the user in making specific data requests. In section 1, the user will be asked to define the resource area, and section 2 generates tables for the specified area. In each section, the user is asked to supply specific options that will serve to customize the database retrieval.

There are four options available for defining the geographic area of interest. Each option provides an increasing level of detail. The region, subregion, State, or county defines an area. The user selects the option that best suits the level of detail required. Users who select county as an option should be aware that some counties have been combined due to data sensitivity. These combined counties are identified with asterisks in the output tables.

The TPO contacts are listed for each region to provide additional explanation or clarification.

Tony Johnson
Southern Research Station
USDA Forest Service
200 W.T. Weaver Blvd.
Asheville, NC 28804
tjohnson09@fs.fed.us
828-257-4888

Helen Beresford
Southern Research Station
USDA Forest Service
4700 Old Kingston Pike
Knoxville, TN 37919
hberesford@fs.fed.us
865-862-2091

James Bentley
Southern Research Station
USDA Forest Service
4700 Old Kingston Pike
Knoxville, TN 37919
jbentley@fs.fed.us
865-862-2056

Carolyn Steppleton
Southern Research Station
USDA Forest Service
200 W.T. Weaver Blvd.
Asheville, NC 28804
csteppleton@fs.fed.us
828-257-4848

Contents

[a] All tables in this report are available in Microsoft® Excel workbook files. Upon request, these files will be supplied in the format the customer requests. The use of trade or firm names in this publication is for reader information and does not imply endorsement by the U.S. Department of Agriculture of any product or service.

Figure 1—Movement of roundwood exports and imports within the United States.

Tennessee's Timber Industry— An Assessment of Timber Product Output and Use, 2009

James W. Bentley, Tony G. Johnson, and Doug Schnabel

Output of Industrial Timber Products

Note: Certain terms used in this bulletin—retained, export, import, production, and receipts—have specialized meanings unique to the Forest Inventory and Analysis Work Units across the country that deal with timber product output (TPO) (fig. 1). Unless otherwise indicated, the context for production and receipts comparisons (increases, decreases, and stabilizations) throughout the report is from 2007 to 2009.

All Products

- Between 2007 and 2009, TPO from roundwood was down 72.0 million cubic feet, or 24 percent, to 225.1 million cubic feet, while output of utilized plant byproducts was down 34.6 million cubic feet to 79.4 million cubic feet.

- Output of softwood roundwood products declined 27 percent to 47.4 million cubic feet, and output of hardwood roundwood products decreased 23 percent to 177.8 million cubic feet (fig. 2).

- Saw logs and pulpwood were the principal roundwood products in 2009. Combined output of these products totaled 221.0 million cubic feet and accounted for 98 percent of Tennessee's total industrial roundwood output (fig. 3).

- Total receipts at Tennessee mills, which included roundwood harvested and retained in the State as well as roundwood imported from other States, decreased by 23 percent to 251.5 million cubic feet. At the same time, the number of primary roundwood-using plants in Tennessee was down from 329 in 2007 to 267 in 2009 (fig. 4).

- Across all products, 71 percent of roundwood harvested was retained for processing at Tennessee mills. Exports of roundwood to other States amounted to 64.7 million cubic feet, while imports of roundwood amounted to 91.1 million cubic feet making the State a net importer of roundwood. Tables A.8 to A.10 show exports to and imports from other States by individual product type.

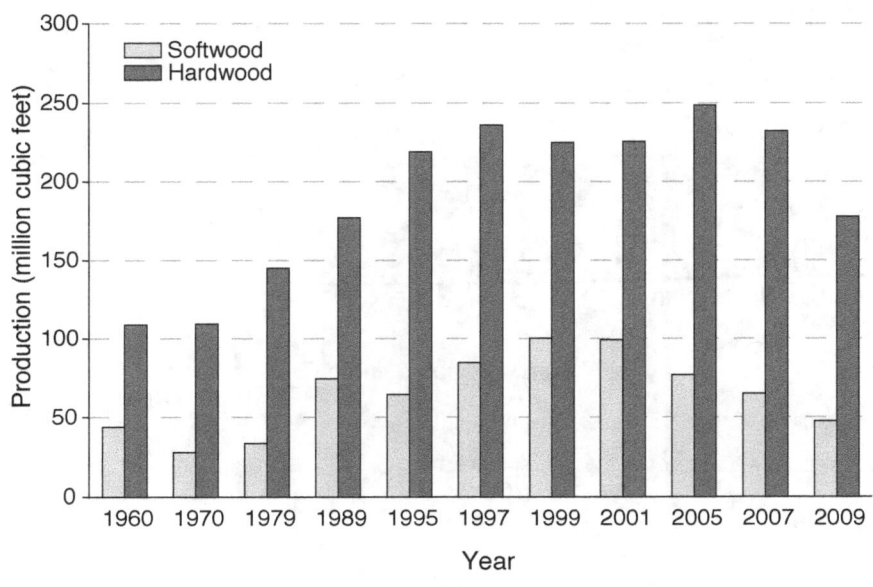

Figure 2—Roundwood production for all products by species group and year (see page 7 for references for individual years), Tennessee.

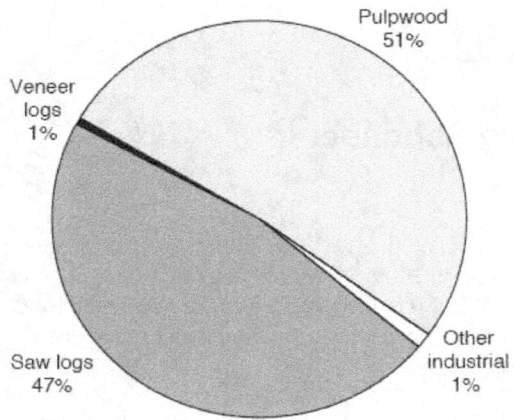

Total 225 million cubic feet

Figure 3—Roundwood production by type of product, Tennessee, 2009.

Saw Logs

- Saw logs accounted for 47 percent of the State's total industrial roundwood products. Output of softwood saw logs declined 40 percent to 8.0 million cubic feet (45 million board feet, International ¼-inch rule), while that of hardwood saw logs was down 36 percent to 97.5 million cubic feet (587 million board feet, International ¼-inch rule) (fig. 5).

- In 2009, Tennessee had 257 sawmills, a loss of 63 mills since 2007. Total saw-log receipts were down 57.7 million cubic feet to 98.9 million cubic feet. Softwood saw-log receipts declined 53 percent to 2.7 million cubic feet, and hardwoods decreased 36 percent to 96.1 million cubic feet. Of the 257 operating mills in 2009, 51 percent, or 131 mills, had receipts of <1 million board feet. Fourteen percent, or 36 mills, had receipts >5 million board feet and accounted for 59 percent of the total saw-log receipts.

- Tennessee retained 88 percent of its saw-log production for in-State manufacture in 2009; saw-log exports amounted to 13.2 million cubic feet, while imports totaled 6.5 million cubic feet.

Primary wood-using mills

- Sawmill (0–5 mmbf) ● Sawmill (>20 mmbf) + Veneer ♦ Plywood mill
● Sawmill (5–20 mmbf) ▲ Composite panel ■ Pulpmill ☆ Other mill

Figure 4—Primary wood-using mills by region, Tennessee, 2009.

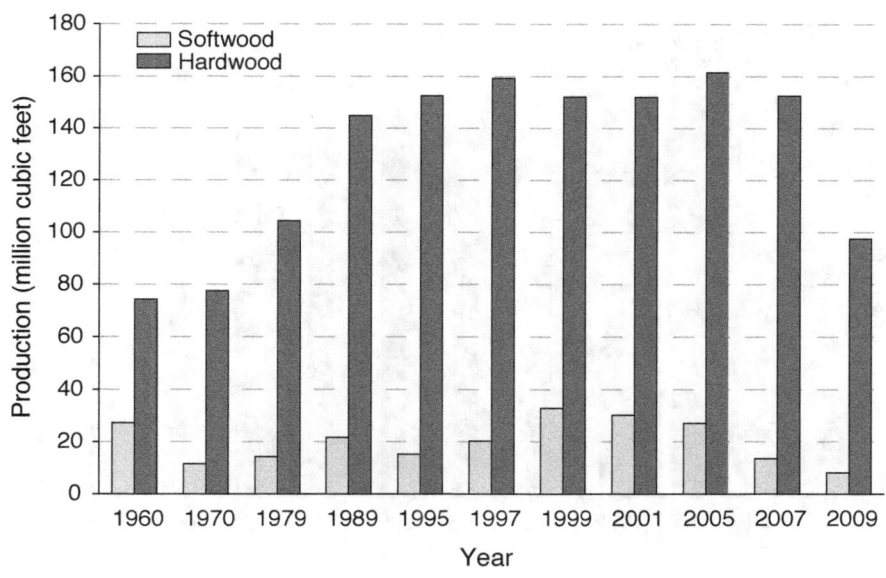

Figure 5—Roundwood saw-log production by species group and year (see page 7 for references for individual years), Tennessee.

Pulpwood

- Total pulpwood production decreased 1.7 million cubic feet to 115.5 million cubic feet and accounted for 51 percent of the State's total industrial roundwood TPO. Softwood output was down 13 percent to 37.6 million cubic feet (518,000 cords); hardwood output increased 6 percent to 77.9 million cubic feet (1.0 million cords) (fig. 6).

- Five pulpmill facilities were operating and receiving roundwood in Tennessee in 2009. Total pulpwood receipts for these mills declined 1.9 million cubic feet to 150.0 million cubic feet, accounting for 60 percent of total receipts for all mills.

- Fifty-seven percent of roundwood cut for pulpwood was retained for processing at Tennessee pulpmills. Roundwood pulpwood accounted for 77 percent of total known exports and 93 percent of total imports. Roundwood pulpwood imports amounted to 84.6 million cubic feet, 34.5 million cubic feet more than was exported.

Veneer Logs

- Output of veneer logs in 2009 totaled 1.3 million cubic feet and accounted for 1 percent of the State's total industrial roundwood TPO volume. Hardwood veneer production decreased 49 percent to 1.2 million cubic feet (8 million board feet, International ¼-inch rule), while softwood veneer production totaled 43,000 cubic feet (255,000 board feet) (fig. 7).

Other Industrial Products

- Roundwood harvested for other industrial uses, such as composite panels, poles, posts, mulch, firewood, logs for log homes, and all other industrial products, was down 76 percent from 11.8 million cubic feet in 2007 to 2.9 million cubic feet in 2009. Softwoods made-up 60 percent of the other industrial product volume.

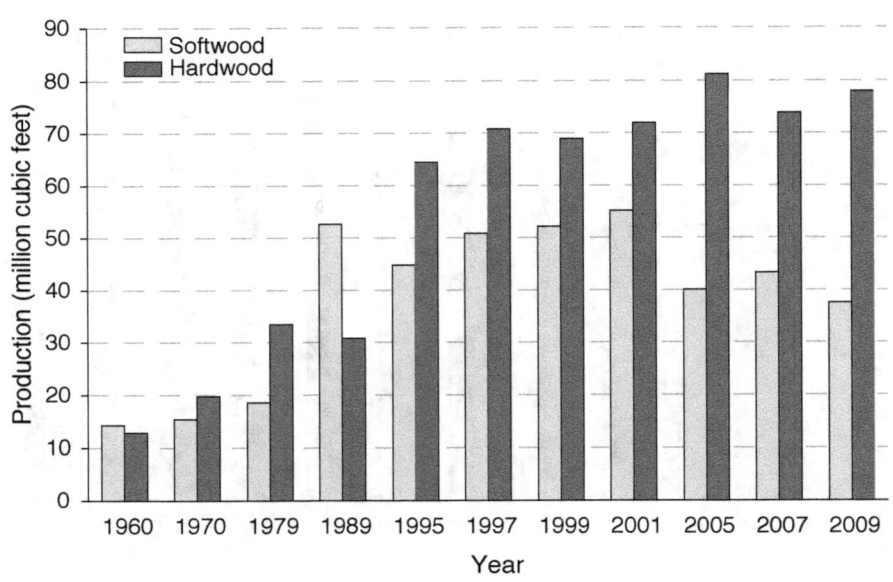

Figure 6—Roundwood pulpwood production by species and year (see page 7 for references for individual years), Tennessee.

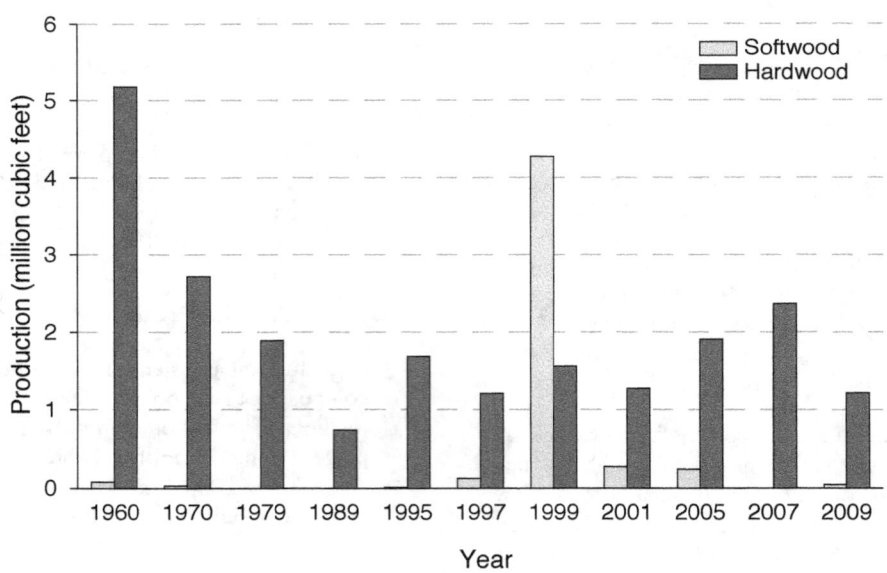

Figure 7—Roundwood veneer-log production by species and year (see page 7 for references for individual years), Tennessee.

Plant Byproducts

- In 2009, processing of primary products in Tennessee mills generated 81.4 million cubic feet of wood and bark residues. Coarse residues from all primary products amounted to 33.9 million cubic feet and bark volume totaled 27.4 million cubic feet. Sawdust and shavings made-up 24 percent of total residues, or 20.1 million cubic feet (fig. 8).

- The processing of saw logs generated 64.2 million cubic feet of mill residues, accounting for 79 percent of the total residues produced (fig. 9).

- Three percent of the wood and bark residues were not used for a product, while 48 percent of the residues were used for industrial fuel (fig. 10). Sixty-five percent, or 21.9 million cubic feet, of the coarse residues were used to manufacture fiber products. Most of the bark was used for industrial fuel or other miscellaneous products, and 65 percent of the sawdust and shavings was used for industrial fuel.

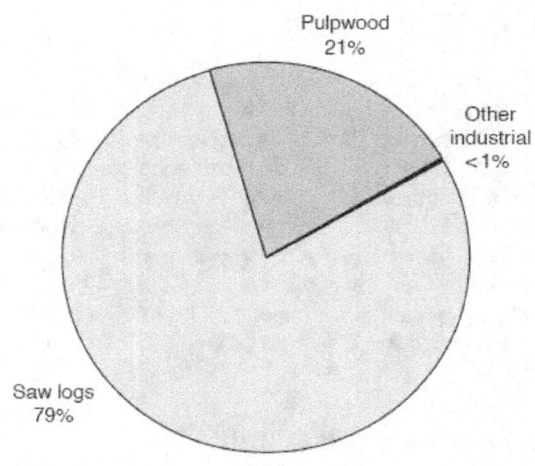

Total 81 million cubic feet

Figure 9—Primary mill residue produced by roundwood type, Tennessee, 2009.

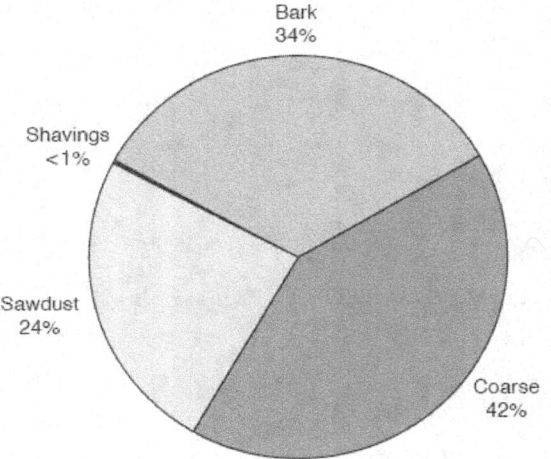

Total 81 million cubic feet

Figure 8—Primary mill residue by residue type, Tennessee, 2009.

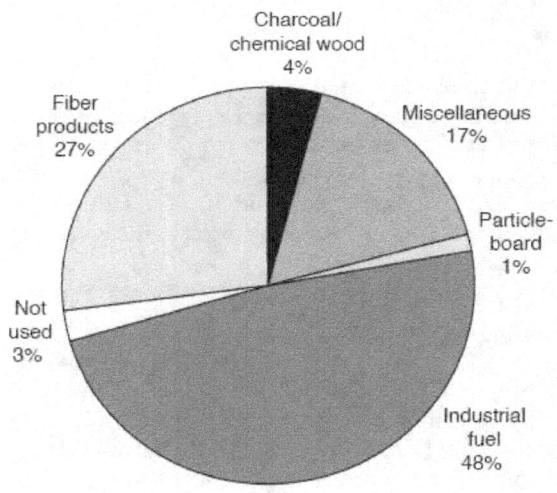

Total 81 million cubic feet

Figure 10—Disposal of residue by product, Tennessee, 2009.

County Data

- Table A.13 shows softwood and hardwood product output by county and individual product type. Out of 95 counties in Tennessee, all had hardwood output; however, 11 of the 95 counties did not have softwood output. Eleven counties (Cumberland, Grundy, Hardeman, Hardin, Hickman, Houston, Lewis, McNairy, Perry, Stewart, and Wayne) had combined softwood and hardwood product output of >5 million cubic feet each. These 11 counties' total product output amounted to 74.6 million cubic feet and accounted for 33 percent of the State's total product output.

Total Roundwood Output

Using the most recent inventory data for Tennessee, product output by source, ownership, and detailed species group was estimated.

Source

- In addition to the 225.1 million cubic feet of roundwood output for industrial products, an estimated 42.6 million cubic feet were harvested for residential fuelwood, bringing Tennessee's total roundwood output to 267.7 million cubic feet.

- Ninety-three percent of total roundwood output was considered growing-stock volume (sawtimber and poletimber) from timberland sources. Other sources (such as saplings; stumps, tops and limbs of trees on timberland; and trees on nonforest land) contributed an estimated 18.9 million cubic feet, or 7 percent of total roundwood output (fig. 11).

Ownership

- An estimated 207.5 million cubic feet, or 78 percent, of the total roundwood output in 2009 came from nonindustrial private forest lands. Forest industry lands contributed 30.5 million cubic feet, or 11 percent of the output. Public lands made-up the remaining 11 percent, or 29.6 million cubic feet (fig. 12).

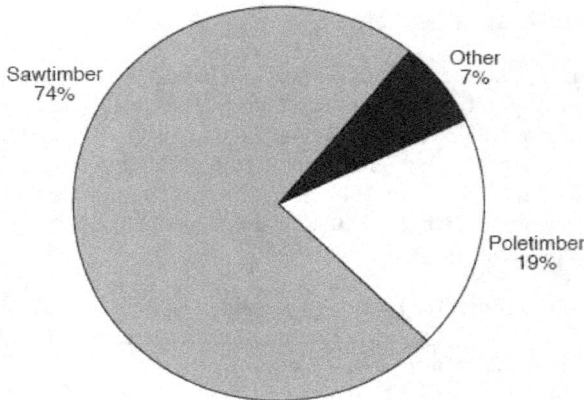

Total 268 million cubic feet

Figure 11—Roundwood output by source, Tennessee, 2009.

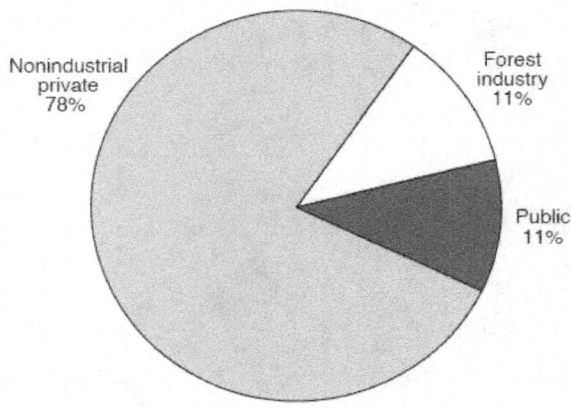

Total 268 million cubic feet

Figure 12—Roundwood output by ownership, Tennessee, 2009.

Species

- The loblolly-shortleaf pine group provided more volume than any other softwood species group, accounting for 69 percent of the total softwood output (fig. 13). The other yellow pine type accounted for another 24 percent of the softwood output. The red oak and white oak groups combined accounted for 110.5 million cubic feet, or 51 percent of total hardwood output (fig. 14).

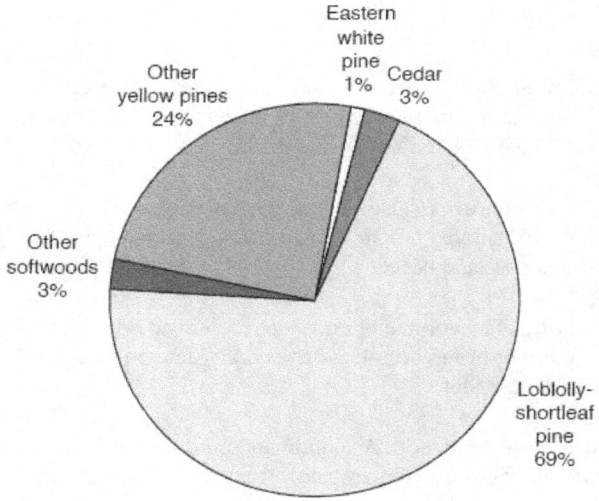

Total 52 million cubic feet

Figure 13—Roundwood output by softwood species group, Tennessee, 2009.

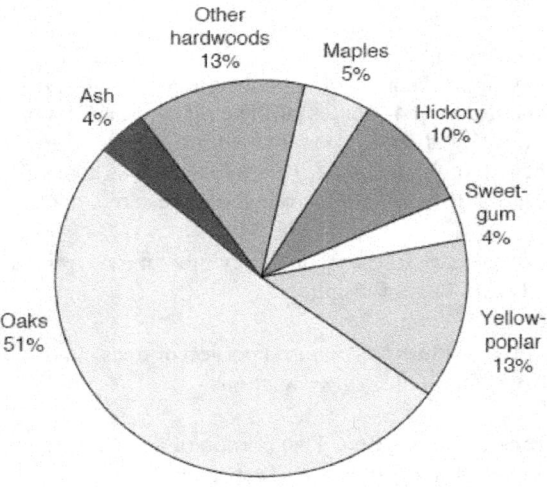

Total 216 million cubic feet

Figure 14—Roundwood output by hardwood species group, Tennessee, 2009.

References

Bentley, J.W.; Schnabel, D. 2007. Tennessee's timber industry—an assessment of timber product output and use, 2005. Resour. Bull. SRS–126. Asheville, NC: U.S. Department of Agriculture Forest Service, Southern Research Station. 31 p. [2005].

Bentley, J.W.; Wright, R.C. 2004. Tennessee's timber industry—an assessment of timber product output and use, 2001. Resour. Bull. SRS–91. Asheville, NC: U.S. Department of Agriculture Forest Service, Southern Research Station. 39 p. [2001].

Bertelson, D.F. 1971. Tennessee forest industries. Resour. Bull. SO–30. New Orleans: U.S. Department of Agriculture Forest Service, Southern Forest Experiment Station. 27 p. [1970].

Howell, M.; Wright, R.C. 2002. Tennessee's timber industry—an assessment of timber product output and use, 1999. Resour. Bull. SRS–76. Asheville, NC: U.S. Department of Agriculture Forest Service, Southern Research Station. 39 p. [1999].

Little, E.L., Jr. 1979. Checklist of United States trees (native and naturalized). Agric. Handb. 541. Washington, DC: U.S. Department of Agriculture. 375 p.

Mathison, R.M.; Schnabel, D. 2009. Tennessee's timber industry—an assessment of timber product output and use, 2007. Resour. Bull. SRS–152. Asheville, NC: U.S. Department of Agriculture Forest Service, Southern Research Station. 29 p. [2007].

Rudis, V.A. 1981. Tennessee forest industries. Resour. Bull. SO–81. New Orleans: U.S. Department of Agriculture Forest Service, Southern Forest Experiment Station. 16 p. [1979].

Sternitzke, H.S. 1962. Tennessee forests. For. Surv. Rel. 86. New Orleans: U.S. Department of Agriculture Forest Service, Southern Forest Experiment Station. 29 p. [1960].

Stratton, D.; Wright, R.C. 1999. Tennessee's timber industry—an assessment of timber product output and use, 1997. Resour. Bull. SRS–42. Asheville, NC: U.S. Department of Agriculture Forest Service, Southern Research Station. 36 p. [1997].

Stratton, D.P.; Wright, R.C. 1998. Tennessee's timber industry—an assessment of timber product output and use, 1995. Resour. Bull. SRS–31. Asheville, NC: U.S. Department of Agriculture Forest Service, Southern Research Station. 21 p. [1995].

Tennessee Valley Authority. 1989. Timber product removals by county and species group. Division of Land and Economic Resources, Forest Resources Development Program. 4 p. Unpublished data. On file with: Southern Research Station, U.S. Department of Agriculture Forest Service, Forest Inventory and Analysis Research Work Unit, 4700 Old Kingston Pike, Knoxville, TN 37919. [1989].

Glossary

Board foot. A unit of measure applied to lumber that is 1-foot long, 1-foot wide, and 1-inch thick (or its equivalent) and also associated with roundwood as to its potential yield of such products.

Byproducts. Primary wood products, e.g., pulp chips, animal bedding, and fuelwood, recycled from mill residues.

Composite panels. Roundwood products manufactured into chips, wafers, strands, flakes, shavings, or sawdust and then reconstituted into a variety of panel and engineered lumber products.

Consumption. The quantity of a commodity, such as pulpwood, utilized by a particular mill or group of mills.

Drain. The volume of roundwood removed from any geographic area where timber is grown.

Exports. The volume of domestic roundwood utilized by mills outside the State where timber was cut.

Fiber products. Byproducts used in the manufacture of pulp, paper, paperboard, and composite products, such as chipboard.

Growing-stock removals. The growing-stock volume removed from poletimber and sawtimber trees in the timberland inventory. (Note: Includes volume removed for roundwood products, logging residues, and other removals.)

Growing-stock trees. Living trees of commercial species classified as sawtimber, poletimber, saplings, and seedlings. Growing-stock trees must contain at least one 12-foot or two 8-foot logs in the saw-log portion, currently or potentially (if too small to qualify). The log(s) must meet dimension and merchantability standards and have, currently or potentially, one-third of the gross board-foot volume in sound wood.

Growing-stock volume. The cubic-foot volume of sound wood in growing-stock trees at least 5.0 inches d.b.h. from a 1-foot stump to a minimum 4.0-inch top d.o.b. of the central stem.

Hardwoods. Dicotyledonous trees, usually broadleaf and deciduous.

Soft hardwoods. Hardwood species with an average specific gravity of ≤0.50, such as gums, yellow-poplar, cottonwoods, red maple, basswoods, and willows.

Hard hardwoods. Hardwood species with an average specific gravity >0.50, such as oaks, hard maples, hickories, and beech.

Imports. The volume of domestic roundwood delivered to a mill or group of mills in a specific State but harvested outside that State.

Industrial fuelwood. A roundwood product, with or without bark, used to generate energy at a manufacturing facility such as a wood-using mill.

Industrial roundwood products. Any primary use of the main stem of a tree, such as saw logs, pulpwood, veneer logs, intended to be processed into primary wood products such as lumber, wood pulp, sheathing, at primary wood-using mills.

International ¼-inch rule. A log rule or formula for estimating the board-foot volume of logs, allowing ½-inch of taper for each 4-foot length. The rule appears in a number of forms that allow for kerf. In the form used by FIA, a ¼-inch of kerf is assumed. This rule is used as the U.S. Forest Service standard log rule in the Eastern United States.

Log. A primary forest product harvested in long, primarily 8-, 12-, and 16-foot lengths.

Logging residues. The unused portion of trees cut or destroyed during logging operations.

Merchantable portion. That portion of live trees 5.0 inches d.b.h. and larger between a 1-foot stump and a minimum 4.0-inch top d.o.b. on the central stem. That portion of primary forks from the point of occurrence to a minimum 4.0-inch top d.o.b. is included.

Merchantable volume. Solid-wood volume in the merchantable portion of live trees.

Noncommercial species. Tree species of typically small size, poor form, or inferior quality that normally do not develop into trees suitable for industrial wood products.

Nonforest land. Land that has never supported forests and land formerly forested where timber production is precluded by development for other uses.

Nongrowing-stock sources. The net volume removed from the nongrowing-stock portions of poletimber and sawtimber trees (stumps, tops, limbs, cull sections of central stem) and from any portion of a rough, rotten, sapling, dead, or nonforest tree.

Other forest land. Forest land other than timberland and productive reserved forest land. It includes available and reserved forest land that is incapable of producing annually 20 cubic feet per acre of industrial wood under natural conditions because of adverse site conditions such as sterile soils, dry climate, poor drainage, high elevation, steepness, or rockiness.

Other products. A miscellaneous category of roundwood products, e.g., cooperage, excelsior, shingles, and mill residue byproducts (charcoal, bedding, mulch, etc.).

Other removals. The growing-stock volume of trees removed from the inventory by cultural operations such as timber stand improvement, land clearing, and other changes in land use, resulting in the removal of the trees from timberland.

Other sources. (See: Nongrowing-stock sources.)

Ownership. The property owned by one ownership unit, including all parcels of land in the United States.

National forest land. Federal land that has been legally designated as national forests or purchase units, and other land under the administration of the Forest Service, including experimental areas and Bankhead-Jones Title III land.

Forest industry land. Land owned by companies or individuals operating primary wood-using plants.

Nonindustrial private forest (NIPF) land. Privately owned land excluding forest industry land.

Corporate. Owned by corporations, including incorporated farm ownerships.

Individual. All lands owned by individuals, including farm operators.

Other public. An ownership class that includes all public lands except national forests.

Miscellaneous Federal land. Federal land other than national forests.

State, county, and municipal land. Land owned by States, counties, and local public agencies or municipalities, or land leased to these governmental units for 50 years or more.

Plant residues. Wood material generated in the production of timber products at primary manufacturing plants.

Coarse residues. Material, such as slabs, edgings, trim, veneer cores and ends, which is suitable for chipping.

Fine residues. Material, such as sawdust, shavings, and veneer residue, which is not suitable for chipping.

Plant byproducts. Residues (coarse or fine) used in the further manufacture of industrial products for consumer use, or as fuel.

Unused plant residues. Residues (coarse or fine) that are not used for any product, including fuel.

Poletimber-size trees. Softwoods 5.0 to 8.9 inches d.b.h. and hardwoods 5.0 to 10.9 inches d.b.h.

Posts, poles, and pilings. Roundwood products milled (cut or peeled) into standard sizes (lengths and circumferences) to be put in the ground to provide vertical and lateral support in buildings, foundations, utility lines, and fences. May also include nonindustrial (unmilled) products.

Primary wood-using plants. Industries that convert round-wood products (saw logs, veneer logs, pulpwood, etc.) into primary wood products, such as lumber, veneer or sheathing, wood pulp.

Production. The total volume of known roundwood harvested from land within a State, regardless of where it is consumed. Production is the sum of timber harvested and used within a State, and all roundwood exported to other States.

Pulpwood. A roundwood product that will be reduced to individual wood fibers by chemical or mechanical means. The fibers are used to make a broad generic group of pulp products that includes paper products, as well as fiberboard, insulating board, and paperboard.

Receipts. The quantity or volume of industrial roundwood received at a mill or by a group of mills in a State, regardless of the geographic source. Volume of roundwood receipts is equal to the volume of roundwood retained in a State plus roundwood imported from other States.

Residental fuelwood. The volume of roundwood harvested to produce heat for residential settings.

Retained. Roundwood volume harvested from and processed by mills within the same State.

Rotten trees. Live trees of commercial species not containing at least one 12-foot saw log, or two noncontiguous saw logs, each 8 feet or longer, now or prospectively, primarily because of rot or missing sections, and with less than one-third of the gross board-foot tree volume in sound material.

Rough trees. Live trees of commercial species not containing at least one 12-foot saw log, or two noncontiguous saw logs, each 8 feet or longer, now or prospectively, primarily because of roughness, poor form, splits, and cracks, and with less than one-third of the gross board-foot tree volume in sound material; and live trees of noncommercial species.

Roundwood (roundwood logs). Logs, bolts, or other round sections cut from trees for industrial manufacture or consumer uses.

Roundwood chipped. Any timber cut primarily for industrial manufacture, delivered to nonpulpmills, chipped, and then sold to pulpmills for use as fiber. Includes tops, jump sections, whole trees, and pulpwood sticks.

Roundwood product drain. That portion of total drain used for a product.

Roundwood products. Any primary product, such as lumber, veneer, composite panels, poles, pilings, pulp, or fuelwood that is produced from roundwood.

Salvable dead trees. Standing or downed dead trees that were formerly growing stock and considered merchantable. Trees must be at least 5.0 inches d.b.h. to qualify.

Saplings. Live trees 1.0 to 5.0 inches d.b.h.

Saw log. A roundwood product, usually 8 feet in length or longer, processed into a variety of sawn products such as lumber, cants, pallets, railroad ties, and timbers.

Saw-log portion. The part of the bole of sawtimber trees between a 1-foot stump and the saw-log top.

Saw-log top. The point on the bole of sawtimber trees above which a conventional saw log cannot be produced. The minimum saw-log top is 7.0 inches d.o.b. for softwoods and 9.0 inches d.o.b. for hardwoods for FIA standards.

Sawtimber-size trees. Softwoods 9.0 inches d.b.h. and larger and hardwoods 11.0 inches d.b.h. and larger.

Sawtimber volume. Growing-stock volume in the saw-log portion of sawtimber-sized trees in board feet (International ¼-inch rule).

Seedlings. Trees < 1.0 inch d.b.h. and > 1 foot tall for hardwoods, > 6 inches tall for softwoods, and > 0.5 inch in diameter at ground level for longleaf pine.

Select red oaks. A group of several red oak species composed of cherrybark, Shumard, and northern red oaks. Other red oak species are included in the "other red oaks" group.

Select white oaks. A group of several white oak species composed of white, swamp chestnut, swamp white, chinkapin, Durand, and bur oaks. Other white oak species are included in the "other white oaks" group.

Softwoods. Coniferous trees, usually evergreen, having leaves that are needles or scale like.

Standard cord. A unit of measure applied to roundwood, usually bolts or split wood. It is a stack of wood 4 feet high, 4 feet wide, and 8 feet long encompassing 128 cubic feet of wood, bark, and air space. This usually translates to approximately 75.0 to 81.0 cubic feet of solid wood for pulpwood, because pulpwood is more uniform.

Standard unit. A unit measure applied to roundwood timber products. Board feet (International ¼-inch rule) is the standard unit used for saw logs and veneer; cords are used for pulpwood, composite panel, and fuelwood; hundred pieces for poles; thousand pieces for posts; and thousand cubic feet for all other miscellaneous forest products.

Timberland. Forest land capable of producing 20 cubic feet of industrial wood per acre per year and not withdrawn from timber utilization.

Timber product output. The total volume of roundwood products from all sources plus the volume of byproducts recovered from mill residues (equals roundwood product drain).

Timber products. Roundwood products and byproducts.

Timber removals. The total volume of trees removed from the timberland inventory by harvesting, cultural operations such as stand improvement, land clearing, or changes in land use. (Note: Includes roundwood products, logging residues, and other removals.)

Tree. Woody plants having one erect perennial stem or trunk at least 3 inches d.b.h., a more or less definitely formed crown of foliage, and a height of at least 13 feet (at maturity).

Upper-stem portion. The part of the main stem of saw-timber trees above the saw-log top and the minimum top diameter of 4.0 inches outside bark, or to the point where the main stem breaks into limbs.

Utilization studies. Studies conducted on active logging operations to develop factors for merchantable portions of trees left in the woods (logging residues), logging damage, and utilization of the unmerchantable portion of growing-stock trees and nongrowing-stock trees.

Veneer log. A roundwood product either rotary cut, sliced, stamped, or sawn into a variety of veneer products such as plywood, finished panels, veneer sheets, or sheathing.

Weight. A unit of measure for mill residues, expressed as oven-dry tons (2,000 oven-dry pounds).

Conversion Factors[a]

Saw logs	
Softwood	0.18018 cubic foot = 1 board foot
	5.55 board feet = 1 cubic foot
Hardwood	0.16556 cubic foot = 1 board foot
	6.04 board feet = 1 cubic foot
Veneer logs	
Softwood	0.17391 cubic foot = 1 board foot
	5.75 board feet = 1 cubic foot
Hardwood	0.15873 cubic foot = 1 board foot
	6.30 board feet = 1 cubic foot
Pulpwood[b]	
Softwood	72.5 cubic feet per cord
Hardwood	76.6 cubic feet per cord

[a] Conversion factors vary with stem size (d.b.h.) and species. The factors shown are for trees of average diameters removed in Tennessee during the most recent survey period.

[b] Cubic feet of solid wood per cord.

Species List[a]

Common name	Scientific name[b]	Common name	Scientific name[b]
Softwoods		**Hardwoods (continued)**	
Southern redcedar	*Juniperus silicicola* (Small) Bailey	Kentucky coffeetree	*Gymnocladus dioicus* (L.) K. Koch
Eastern redcedar	*J. virginiana* L.	Silverbell	*Halesia* Ellis ex L.
Shortleaf pine	*Pinus echinata* Mill.	American holly	*Ilex opaca* Ait.
Table Mt. pine	*P. pungens* Lamb.	Butternut	*Juglans cinerea* L.
Pitch pine	*P. rigida* Mill.	(white walnut)	
Eastern white pine	*P. strobus* L.	Black walnut	*J. nigra* L.
Loblolly pine	*P. taeda* L.	Sweetgum	*Liquidambar styraciflua* L.
Virginia pine	*P. virginiana* Mill.	Yellow-poplar	*Liriodendron tulipifera* L.
Baldcypress	*Taxodium distichum* (L.) Rich.	Osage orange	*Maclura pomifera* (Raf.) Schneid.
Eastern hemlock	*Tsuga canadensis* (L.) Carr.	Cucumbertree	*Magnolia acuminata* L.
		Southern magnolia	*M. grandiflora* L.
Hardwoods		Bigleaf magnolia	*M. macrophylla* Michx.
Florida maple	*Acer barbatum* Michx.	Apple	*Malus* spp. Mill.
Boxelder	*A. negundo* L.	Chinaberry	*Melia azedarach* L.
Striped maple	*A. pensylvanicum* L.	White mulberry	*Morus alba* L.
Red maple	*A. rubrum* L.	Red mulberry	*M. rubra* L.
Silver maple	*A. saccharinum* L.	Water tupelo	*Nyssa aquatica* L.
Sugar maple	*A. saccharum* Marsh.	Blackgum	*N. sylvatica* Marsh.
Buckeye	*Aesculus* spp. L.	Swamp tupelo	*N. sylvatica* var. *biflora* (Walt.) Sarg.
Yellow buckeye	*A. octandra* Marsh.	Eastern hophornbeam	*Ostrya virginiana* (Mill.) K. Koch
Ailanthus	*Ailanthus altissima* (Mill.) Swingle	Sourwood	*Oxydendrum arboreum* (L.) DC.
Serviceberry	*Amelanchier* spp. Medic.	Red spruce	*Picea rubens* Sarg.
Pawpaw	*Asimina* Adans.	American sycamore	*Platanus occidentalis* L.
River birch	*Betula nigra* L.	Cottonwood	*Populus* spp. L.
American hornbeam	*Carpinus caroliniana* Walt.	Black cherry	*Prunus serotina* Ehrh.
Hickory	*Carya* spp. Nutt.	White oak	*Quercus alba* L.
Sand hickory	*C. pallida* (Ashe) Engl. & Graebn.	Scarlet oak	*Q. coccinea* Muenchh.
Water hickory	*C. aquatica* (Michx. f.) Nutt.	Southern red oak	*Q. falcata* Michx.
Bitternut hickory	*C. cordiformis* (Wangenh.) K. Koch	Cherrybark oak	*Q. falcata* var. *pagodifolia* Ell.
Pignut hickory	*C. glabra* (Mill.) Sweet	Overcup oak	*Q. lyrata* Walt.
Pecan	*C. illinoensis* (Wangenh.) K. Koch	Swamp chestnut oak	*Q. michauxii* Nutt.
Shellbark hickory	*C. laciniosa* (Michx. f.) Loud.	Chinkapin oak	*Q. muehlenbergii* Engelm.
Shagbark hickory	*C. ovata* (Mill.) K. Koch	Water oak	*Q. nigra* L.
Mockernut hickory	*C. tomentosa* (Poir.) Nutt.	Pin oak	*Q. palustris* Muenchh.
American chestnut	*Castanea dentata* (Marsh.) Borkh.	Willow oak	*Q. phellos* L.
Allegheny chinkapin	*C. pumila* Mill.	Chestnut oak	Q. *prinus* L.
Chinkapin	*Castanopsis* (D. Don) Spach	Northern red oak	*Q. rubra* L.
Catalpa	*Catalpa* spp. Scop.	Shumard oak	*Q. shumardii* Buckl.
Sugarberry	*Celtis laevigata* Willd.	Post oak	*Q. stellata* Wangenh.
Hackberry	*C. occidentalis* L.	Black oak	*Q. velutina* Lam.
Eastern redbud	*Cercis canadensis* L.	Black locust	*Robinia pseudoacacia* L.
Flowering dogwood	*Cornus florida* L.	Willow	*Salix* spp. L.
Hawthorn	*Crataegus spp.* L.	Sassafras	*Sassafras albidum* (Nutt.) Nees
Common persimmon	*Diospyros virginiana* L.	American basswood	*Tilia americana* L.
American beech	*Fagus grandifolia* Ehrh.	White basswood	*T. heterophylla* Vent.
White ash	*Fraxinus americana* L.	Winged elm	*Ulmus alata* Michx.
Carolina ash	*F. caroliniana* Mill.	American elm	*U. americana* L.
Green ash	*F. pennsylvanica* Marsh.	Slippery elm	*U. rubra* Muhl.
Pumpkin ash	*F. profunda (Bush)* Bush	Rock elm	*U. thomasii* Sarg.
Waterlocust	*Gleditsia aquatica* Marsh.		
Honeylocust	*G. triacanthos* L.		

[a] Common and scientific names of tree species >1 0 inch d.b.h. occurring in the FIA sample.
[b] Little (1979).

Appendix

Index of Tables

Table A.1—Output of industrial products by product and species group, Tennessee, 2007 and 2009

Product and species group	Year 2007	Year 2009	Change	Change
	- - - - thousand cubic feet - - - -			percent
Saw logs				
Softwood	13,448	8,029	-5,419	-40.3
Hardwood	152,316	97,450	-54,866	-36.0
Total	165,764	105,479	-60,285	-36.4
Veneer logs				
Softwood	0	43	43	—
Hardwood	2,365	1,218	-1,147	-48.5
Total	2,365	1,261	-1,104	-46.7
Pulpwood				
Softwood	43,360	37,571	-5,789	-13.4
Hardwood	73,834	77,945	4,111	5.6
Total	117,194	115,516	-1,678	-1.4
Other industrial[a]				
Softwood	8,218	1,722	-6,496	-79.0
Hardwood	3,565	1,155	-2,410	-67.6
Total	11,783	2,877	-8,906	-75.6
All industrial				
Softwood	65,026	47,365	-17,661	-27.2
Hardwood	232,080	177,768	-54,312	-23.4
Total	297,106	225,133	-71,973	-24.2

[a] Includes posts, poles, and composite panels.

Table A.2—Roundwood receipts by product and species group, Tennessee, 2007 and 2009

Product and species group	Year 2007	Year 2009	Change	Change
	- - - - thousand cubic feet - - - -			percent
Saw logs				
Softwood	5,815	2,739	-3,076	-52.9
Hardwood	150,802	96,137	-54,665	-36.2
Total	156,617	98,876	-57,741	-36.9
Pulpwood				
Softwood	98,832	83,073	-15,759	-15.9
Hardwood	53,123	66,945	13,822	26.0
Total	151,955	150,018	-1,937	-1.3
Other industrial[ab]				
Softwood	12,950	1,481	-11,469	-88.6
Hardwood	5,543	1,169	-4,374	-78.9
Total	18,493	2,650	-15,843	-85.7
Total output				
Softwood	117,597	87,293	-30,304	-25.8
Hardwood	209,468	164,251	-45,217	-21.6
Total	327,065	251,544	-75,521	-23.1

[a] Includes posts, poles, veneer logs, and composite panels.
[b] Includes 685,000 cubic feet used as industrial fuel in 2009.

Table A.3—Number of primary wood-using plants by type of mill, Tennessee, 1960 to 2009

Type of mill	1960	1970	1979	1989	1995	1997	1999	2001	2005	2007	2009
						number					
Sawmills	1,135	546	694	490	495	496	440	439	345	320	257
Veneer mills	9	6	5	3	2	2	2	2	1	1	1
Pulpmills	5	7	7	6	5	5	5	5	5	5	5
Composite panel mills	0	0	0	0	0	1	1	1	1	1	1
Other mills	133	64	32	24	1	1	3	3	2	2	3
All plants	1,282	623	738	523	503	505	451	450	354	329	267

Table A.4—Roundwood receipts by sawmill size, Tennessee, 2007 and 2009

Sawmill size class[a]	2007			2009		
	Mills	Volume		Mills	Volume	
mmbf	*number*	*mbf*	*percent*	*number*	*mbf*	*percent*
< 1.0	147	46,867	5	131	39,079	7
1.0–4.99	113	282,633	30	90	203,512	34
5.0–9.99	36	249,029	26	24	175,068	29
> 10.0	24	362,568	39	12	177,067	30
Total	320	941,097	100	257	594,726	100

[a] Based on volume received as opposed to actual capacity.

Table A.5—Roundwood receipts by species and type of mill, Tennessee, 2009

Species	All mills	Type of mill		
		Sawmills	Pulpmills	Other mills[a][b]
		thousand cubic feet		
Softwood				
Yellow pine	1,959	1,316	NA	643
Eastern white pine	712	407	NA	305
Cedar	945	413	NA	532
Cypress	518	517	NA	1
Other softwood	86	86	NA	0
Unclassified	83,073	0	83,073	0
Total softwoods	87,293	2,739	83,073	1,481
Hardwood				
Blackgum and tupelo	568	554	NA	14
Soft maple	1,740	1,712	NA	28
Sweetgum	3,720	3,692	NA	28
Yellow-poplar	20,947	20,854	NA	93
Other soft hardwood	2,017	1,594	NA	423
Hickory	6,894	6,847	NA	47
Red oak	25,690	25,556	NA	134
White oak	24,634	24,510	NA	124
Other hard hardwood	11,096	10,818	NA	278
Unclassified	66,945	0	66,945	0
Total hardwoods	164,251	96,137	66,945	1,169
All species	251,544	98,876	150,018	2,650

NA = not applicable.

[a] Includes posts, poles, veneer logs, and composite panels.

[b] Includes 685,000 cubic feet used as industrial fuel in 2009.

Table A.6—Industrial roundwood movement by year and species group, Tennessee, 2007 and 2009

Year	Production	Exported to other States	Retained	Imported from other States	Receipts
		thousand cubic feet			
		Softwood			
2007	65,026	15,985	49,041	68,556	117,597
2009	47,365	13,705	33,660	53,633	87,293
		Hardwood			
2007	232,080	64,356	167,724	41,744	209,468
2009	177,768	50,995	126,773	37,478	164,251
		All species			
2007	297,106	80,341	216,765	110,300	327,065
2009	225,133	64,700	160,433	91,111	251,544

Table A.7—Industrial roundwood movement by product and species group, Tennessee, 2009

Product and species group	Production	Exported to other States	Retained	Imported from other States	Receipts
		thousand cubic feet			
Saw logs					
Softwood	8,029	5,395	2,634	105	2,739
Hardwood	97,450	7,756	89,694	6,443	96,137
Total	105,479	13,151	92,328	6,548	98,876
Pulpwood					
Softwood	37,571	8,017	29,554	53,519	83,073
Hardwood	77,945	42,033	35,912	31,033	66,945
Total	115,516	50,050	65,466	84,552	150,018
Other industrial[a]					
Softwood	1,765	293	1,472	9	1,481
Hardwood	2,373	1,206	1,167	2	1,169
Total	4,138	1,499	2,639	11	2,650
All products					
Softwood	47,365	13,705	33,660	53,633	87,293
Hardwood	177,768	50,995	126,773	37,478	164,251
Total	225,133	64,700	160,433	91,111	251,544

[a] Includes posts, poles, veneer logs, and composite panels.

Table A.8—Saw-log volume by destination, source, and species group, Tennessee, 2009

Destination and source	All species	Species group	
		Softwood	Hardwood
	thousand cubic feet		
Tennessee (retained)	92,328	2,634	89,694
Exports to			
Alabama	563	231	332
Georgia	1,083	677	406
Indiana	49	0	49
Kentucky	5,581	354	5,227
Mississippi	4,192	3,899	293
Missouri	914	144	770
North Carolina	522	90	432
Virginia	247	0	247
Total	13,151	5,395	7,756
Imports from			
Alabama	3,944	1	3,943
Arkansas	60	43	17
Kentucky	1,066	7	1,059
Mississippi	1,099	30	1,069
North Carolina	114	24	90
Virginia	265	0	265
Total	6,548	105	6,443

Table A.9—Pulpwood volume by destination, source, and species group, Tennessee, 2009

Destination and source	All species	Species group	
		Softwood	Hardwood
	thousand cubic feet		
Tennessee (retained)	65,466	29,554	35,912
Exports to			
Alabama	31,897	6,054	25,843
Arkansas	27	0	27
Georgia	16	16	0
Kentucky	9,630	1,947	7,683
North Carolina	8,444	0	8,444
South Carolina	33	0	33
Virginia	3	0	3
Total	50,050	8,017	42,033
Imports from			
Alabama	9,598	8,293	1,305
Georgia	22,357	14,823	7,534
Kentucky	6,495	1,336	5,159
Mississippi	31,487	27,932	3,555
North Carolina	6,236	764	5,472
South Carolina	442	371	71
Virginia	7,937	0	7,937
Total	84,552	53,519	31,033

Table A.10—Other industrial[a] volume by destination, source, and species group, Tennessee, 2009

Destination and source	All species	Species group	
		Softwood	Hardwood
	thousand cubic feet		
Tennessee (retained)	2,639	1,472	1,167
Exports to			
Georgia	490	0	490
Indiana	58	1	57
Kentucky	251	250	1
Michigan	81	0	81
North Carolina	538	42	496
Virginia	81	0	81
Total	1,499	293	1,206
Imports from			
Georgia	11	9	2
Total	11	9	2

[a] Includes posts, poles, veneer logs, and composite panels.

Table A.11—Primary mill residue volume by roundwood type, species group, and residue type, Tennessee, 2009

Roundwood type and species group	All types	Residue type			
		Bark	Coarse	Sawdust	Shavings
	thousand cubic feet				
Saw logs					
Softwood	1,525	187	819	492	27
Hardwood	62,638	9,968	33,114	19,356	200
Total	64,163	10,155	33,933	19,848	227
Pulpwood					
Softwood	8,611	8,611	0	0	0
Hardwood	8,439	8,439	0	0	0
Total	17,050	17,050	0	0	0
Other industrial[a]					
Softwood	100	100	0	0	0
Hardwood	82	56	15	11	0
Total	182	156	15	11	0
Total					
Softwood	10,236	8,898	819	492	27
Hardwood	71,159	18,463	33,129	19,367	200
Total	81,395	27,361	33,948	19,859	227

[a] Includes poles, pilings, posts, composite panels, veener logs, and other industrial products.

Table A.12—Disposal of residue at primary wood-using plants by product, species group, and type of residue, Tennessee, 2007 and 2009

Product and species group	All types 2007	All types 2009	Bark 2007	Bark 2009	Coarse 2007	Coarse 2009	Sawdust 2007	Sawdust 2009	Shavings 2007	Shavings 2009
					thousand cubic feet					
Fiber products										
Softwood	947	281	0	0	947	281	0	0	0	0
Hardwood	33,877	21,647	0	0	33,877	21,647	0	0	0	0
Total	34,824	21,928	0	0	34,824	21,928	0	0	0	0
Particleboard										
Softwood	53	0	0	0	38	0	15	0	0	0
Hardwood	3,702	1,138	0	0	2,993	1,078	687	60	22	0
Total	3,755	1,138	0	0	3,031	1,078	702	60	22	0
Charcoal/ chemical wood										
Softwood	90	39	0	1	63	38	27	0	0	0
Hardwood	3,709	3,416	44	479	1,264	1,342	2,401	1,595	0	0
Total	3,799	3,455	44	480	1,327	1,380	2,428	1,595	0	0
Sawn products										
Softwood	1	0	0	0	1	0	0	0	0	0
Hardwood	8	0	0	0	8	0	0	0	0	0
Total	9	0	0	0	9	0	0	0	0	0
Industrial fuel										
Softwood	13,263	9,107	12,571	8,727	170	144	518	236	4	0
Hardwood	37,160	30,189	11,642	11,655	4,425	5,713	20,852	12,724	241	97
Total	50,423	39,296	24,213	20,382	4,595	5,857	21,370	12,960	245	97
Miscellaneous										
Softwood	1,211	682	401	150	312	279	417	227	81	26
Hardwood	19,938	12,866	10,408	5,968	4,436	2,568	4,772	4,261	322	69
Total	21,149	13,548	10,809	6,118	4,748	2,847	5,189	4,488	403	95
Not used										
Softwood	296	127	44	20	194	77	57	29	1	1
Hardwood	8,293	1,903	1,632	361	4,983	781	1,664	727	14	34
Total	8,589	2,030	1,676	381	5,177	858	1,721	756	15	35
All products										
Softwood	15,861	10,236	13,016	8,898	1,725	819	1,034	492	86	27
Hardwood	106,687	71,159	23,726	18,463	51,986	33,129	30,376	19,367	599	200
Total	122,548	81,395	36,742	27,361	53,711	33,948	31,410	19,859	685	227

Table A.13—Roundwood timber product output by county, product, and species group, Tennessee, 2009

County	All products Soft-wood	All products Hard-wood	Saw logs Soft-wood	Saw logs Hard-wood	Veneer logs Soft-wood	Veneer logs Hard-wood	Pulpwood Soft-wood	Pulpwood Hard-wood	Other industrial[a] Soft-wood	Other industrial[a] Hard-wood
					thousand cubic feet					
Anderson	8	2,370	0	1,300	0	88	8	982	0	0
Bedford	47	521	47	488	0	0	0	33	0	0
Benton	487	1,202	39	678	0	0	445	507	3	17
Bledsoe	781	2,901	7	526	0	0	774	2,375	0	0
Blount	172	533	0	221	0	0	172	312	0	0
Bradley	756	863	329	474	0	0	427	389	0	0
Campbell	112	4,322	111	1,538	0	0	1	2,784	0	0
Cannon	33	983	7	976	0	0	0	7	26	0
Carroll	910	2,119	95	1,201	0	0	813	880	2	38
Carter	42	572	42	449	0	122	0	1	0	0
Cheatham	0	1,489	0	1,489	0	0	0	0	0	0
Chester	1,480	1,758	709	1,107	0	0	771	651	0	0
Claiborne	6	2,852	6	1,508	0	0	0	1,344	0	0
Clay	34	1,065	11	1,063	0	0	0	0	23	2
Cocke	82	1,256	82	698	0	81	0	477	0	0
Coffee	84	865	0	616	0	0	84	249	0	0
Cumberland	197	5,510	7	890	0	0	143	4,604	47	16
Davidson	0	106	0	106	0	0	0	0	0	0
Decatur	1,300	2,220	0	962	0	0	1,300	1,258	0	0
DeKalb	225	809	95	793	0	0	0	16	130	0
Dickson	0	3,303	0	1,963	0	0	0	1,340	0	0
Dyer	119	463	50	410	0	0	69	53	0	0
Fayette	67	1,160	0	928	0	0	67	232	0	0
Fentress	427	1,591	85	766	0	0	229	825	113	0
Franklin	16	3,001	13	1,918	0	44	3	1,039	0	0
Gibson	24	618	22	457	0	0	1	161	1	0
Giles	477	3,879	37	2,958	0	0	440	921	0	0
Grainger	0	1,610	0	1,605	0	0	0	5	0	0
Greene	11	872	8	864	0	0	3	8	0	0
Grundy	1,207	4,360	38	1,056	0	0	1,150	3,298	19	6
Hamblen	0	231	0	231	0	0	0	0	0	0
Hamilton	1,095	841	145	355	0	0	950	486	0	0
Hancock	0	782	0	782	0	0	0	0	0	0
Hardeman	2,145	3,163	966	1,275	0	0	1,179	1,888	0	0
Hardin	4,514	3,061	896	1,922	0	0	3,618	1,139	0	0
Hawkins	35	1,868	1	443	34	374	0	952	0	99
Haywood	21	569	20	452	0	0	1	117	0	0
Henderson	1,057	2,059	0	870	0	0	1,057	1,189	0	0
Henry	380	2,192	102	1,812	0	0	275	308	3	72
Hickman	445	5,583	11	2,500	0	0	434	3,083	0	0
Houston	12	5,596	0	2,113	0	0	12	3,325	0	158
Humphreys	792	3,707	0	2,700	0	0	792	1,007	0	0
Jackson	95	2,358	95	2,345	0	0	0	13	0	0
Jefferson	2	340	2	96	0	0	0	244	0	0
Johnson	132	710	132	515	0	0	0	195	0	0
Knox	154	429	5	378	0	44	149	7	0	0
Lake	72	104	72	104	0	0	0	0	0	0
Lauderdale	0	57	0	57	0	0	0	0	0	0

continued

Table A.13—Roundwood timber product output by county, product, and species group, Tennessee, 2009 (continued)

County	All products		Saw logs		Veneer logs		Pulpwood		Other industrial[a]	
	Soft-wood	Hard-wood	Soft-wood	Hard-wood	Soft-wood	Hard-wood	Soft-wood	Hard-wood	Soft-wood	Hard-wood
					thousand cubic feet					
Lawrence	871	3,894	0	2,345	0	0	871	1,549	0	0
Lewis	1,562	8,286	31	1,892	0	0	1,531	6,184	0	210
Lincoln	114	1,455	114	1,080	0	0	0	375	0	0
Loudon	9	379	0	87	0	0	9	292	0	0
Macon	55	3,729	55	3,654	0	0	0	75	0	0
Madison	868	2,151	654	1,422	0	0	214	729	0	0
Marion	462	3,211	0	515	0	0	434	2,686	28	10
Marshall	92	237	92	99	0	0	0	138	0	0
Maury	11	1,315	3	1,197	0	0	8	118	0	0
McMinn	1,583	2,066	47	769	0	44	1,431	1,216	105	37
McNairy	2,658	3,961	869	2,103	0	0	1,789	1,858	0	0
Meigs	279	251	2	245	0	0	258	0	19	6
Monroe	1,150	1,568	95	494	8	70	847	934	200	70
Montgomery	379	951	0	866	1	56	378	29	0	0
Moore	18	529	18	382	0	0	0	147	0	0
Morgan	226	2,339	63	1,117	0	0	144	1,216	19	6
Obion	169	1,504	118	1,206	0	0	51	298	0	0
Overton	401	2,776	202	2,383	0	0	67	387	132	6
Perry	546	5,311	12	2,693	0	0	534	2,618	0	0
Pickett	61	1,153	61	1,153	0	0	0	0	0	0
Polk	738	1,188	282	361	0	0	456	827	0	0
Putnam	245	1,807	178	1,501	0	0	67	306	0	0
Rhea	1,339	1,593	0	503	0	15	1,062	978	277	97
Roane	219	849	1	223	0	0	46	566	172	60
Robertson	0	678	0	678	0	0	0	0	0	0
Rutherford	0	139	0	70	0	0	0	69	0	0
Scott	79	4,426	79	1,938	0	0	0	2,488	0	0
Sequatchie	1,007	788	11	309	0	0	958	466	38	13
Sevier	75	284	0	210	0	0	75	74	0	0
Shelby	870	885	0	814	0	0	870	71	0	0
Smith	436	874	176	874	0	0	0	0	260	0
Stewart	3,192	1,810	0	1,045	0	0	3,192	765	0	0
Sullivan	43	576	43	532	0	44	0	0	0	0
Sumner	0	1,914	0	1,914	0	0	0	0	0	0
Tipton	21	566	6	566	0	0	15	0	0	0
Trousdale	0	304	0	304	0	0	0	0	0	0
Unicoi	97	833	97	668	0	118	0	47	0	0
Union	90	374	0	175	0	0	90	199	0	0
Van Buren	612	3,958	26	1,033	0	0	586	2,925	0	0
Warren	196	2,422	132	1,450	0	0	64	972	0	0
Washington	18	3,117	18	701	0	118	0	2,079	0	219
Wayne	5,818	5,698	3	1,991	0	0	5,815	3,707	0	0
Weakley	391	2,149	182	1,675	0	0	208	461	1	13
White	130	3,819	0	2,811	0	0	130	1,008	0	0
Williamson	5	645	1	261	0	0	4	384	0	0
Wilson	175	183	71	183	0	0	0	0	104	0
All counties	47,365	177,768	8,029	97,450	43	1,218	37,571	77,945	1,722	1,155

[a] Includes posts, poles, and composite panels.

Table A.14—Total roundwood output by product, species group, and source of material, Tennessee, 2009

| Product and species group | All sources | Total | Growing-stock trees | | Other sources |
			Sawtimber	Poletimber	
			thousand cubic feet		
Saw logs					
Softwood	8,029	7,828	7,402	426	201
Hardwood	97,450	95,169	89,458	5,711	2,281
Total	105,479	102,997	96,860	6,137	2,482
Veneer logs and bolts					
Softwood	43	42	42	0	1
Hardwood	1,218	1,197	1,197	0	21
Total	1,261	1,239	1,239	0	22
Pulpwood					
Softwood	37,571	34,726	21,698	13,028	2,845
Hardwood	77,945	72,013	47,142	24,871	5,932
Total	115,516	106,739	68,840	37,899	8,777
Poles and posts					
Softwood	10	7	4	3	3
Hardwood	140	28	11	17	112
Total	150	35	15	20	115
Other miscellaneous					
Softwood	1,712	1,492	861	631	220
Hardwood	1,015	846	329	517	169
Total	2,727	2,338	1,190	1,148	389
Total industrial products					
Softwood	47,365	44,095	30,007	14,088	3,270
Hardwood	177,768	169,253	138,137	31,116	8,515
Total	225,133	213,348	168,144	45,204	11,785
Residential fuelwood					
Softwood	4,703	4,185	3,098	1,087	518
Hardwood	37,867	31,283	26,224	5,059	6,584
Total	42,570	35,468	29,322	6,146	7,102
All products					
Softwood	52,068	48,280	33,105	15,175	3,788
Hardwood	215,635	200,536	164,361	36,175	15,099
Total	267,703	248,816	197,466	51,350	18,887

Numbers in rows and columns may not sum to totals due to rounding.

Table A.15—Total roundwood output by species group, survey region, and ownership class, Tennessee, 2009

Species group and survey region	Total	Ownership class		
		Public	Forest industry	Nonindustrial private
		thousand cubic feet		
Softwoods				
West	12,372	1,167	1,445	9,760
West Central	21,480	3,671	6,329	11,480
Central	2,503	551	0	1,952
Plateau	6,771	1,768	2,651	2,352
East	8,942	316	429	8,197
Total softwoods	52,068	7,474	10,854	33,740
Hardwoods				
West	30,906	5,812	354	24,741
West Central	56,245	8,829	5,112	42,305
Central	34,365	1,647	436	32,281
Plateau	58,691	5,410	13,474	39,807
East	35,428	470	300	34,658
Total hardwoods	215,635	22,168	19,676	173,791
All species	267,703	29,642	30,530	207,531

Numbers in rows and columns may not sum to totals due to rounding.

Table A.16—Total roundwood output by species group, detailed species group, and product, Tennessee, 2009

Species group and detailed species group	Total	Saw logs	Veneer logs	Pulpwood	Poles and posts	Other miscellaneous	Residential fuelwood
				thousand cubic feet			
Softwood							
Cedar	1,285	304	0	785	0	80	115
Eastern white pine	594	265	0	267	1	7	53
Loblolly-shortleaf pine	36,049	6,250	32	25,820	7	681	3,259
Other yellow pines	12,680	1,130	6	9,558	2	839	1,143
Cypress	781	18	0	693	0	0	70
Hemlock	680	61	4	448	0	105	61
Total softwoods	52,068	8,029	43	37,571	10	1,712	4,703
Hardwood							
Soft maple	5,228	2,773	131	1,389	5	13	918
Hard maple	6,423	2,155	1	3,091	1	47	1,128
Other birch	60	31	0	19	0	0	10
Yellow birch	1,303	342	48	637		48	229
Hickory	20,960	8,660	114	8,234	2	269	3,681
Beech	3,026	1,816	3	676	0	0	531
Ash	8,376	5,341	27	1,520	9	8	1,471
Black walnut	4,992	3,028	17	1,068	1	2	877
Sweetgum	7,652	4,459	15	1,769	42	23	1,344
Yellow-poplar	27,905	14,728	152	8,008	13	103	4,900
Blackgum-tupelo	2,326	858	7	1,038	1	13	408
Sycamore	3,396	1,846	122	826	0	6	597
Cottonwood	1,310	576	0	503	0	0	230
Black cherry	2,686	1,397	14	773	1	29	472
Select white oaks	41,651	16,421	185	17,438	12	280	7,314
Other white oaks	21,790	9,080	116	8,723	4	41	3,826
Select red oaks	12,297	4,850	3	5,251	18	16	2,159
Other red oaks	34,721	13,770	242	14,489	26	96	6,098
Basswood	544	426	0	22	0	0	96
Elm	2,867	1,546	10	798	4	6	503
Other eastern hardwoods	6,123	3,345	13	1,675	1	14	1,076
Total hardwoods	215,635	97,450	1,218	77,945	140	1,015	37,867
All species	267,703	105,479	1,261	115,516	150	2,727	42,570

Numbers in rows and columns may not sum to totals due to rounding.

Table A.17 — Total roundwood output by species group, detailed species group, and ownership class, Tennessee, 2009

Species group and detailed species group	Total	Ownership class		
		Public	Forest industry	Nonindustrial private
		thousand cubic feet		
Softwood				
Cedar	1,285	127	47	1,111
Eastern white pine	594	27	34	533
Loblolly-shortleaf pine	36,049	6,013	7,094	22,942
Other yellow pines	12,680	1,244	3,678	7,757
Cypress	781	34	0	747
Hemlock	680	28	1	650
Total softwoods	52,068	7,474	10,854	33,740
Hardwood				
Soft maple	5,228	613	636	3,979
Hard maple	6,423	1,306	1,747	3,370
Other birch	60	2	1	57
Yellow birch	1,303	36	0	1,267
Hickory	20,960	3,011	1,059	16,890
Beech	3,026	249	76	2,701
Ash	8,376	676	174	7,526
Black walnut	4,992	204	334	4,454
Sweetgum	7,652	1,145	159	6,348
Yellow-poplar	27,905	1,780	2,338	23,787
Blackgum-tupelo	2,326	158	256	1,912
Sycamore	3,396	504	54	2,838
Cottonwood	1,310	246	8	1,055
Black cherry	2,686	181	224	2,282
Select white oaks	41,651	4,861	2,840	33,950
Other white oaks	21,790	1,331	3,619	16,841
Select red oaks	12,297	1,673	1,459	9,166
Other red oaks	34,721	2,984	4,164	27,572
Basswood	544	5	5	534
Elm	2,867	262	235	2,371
Other eastern hardwoods	6,123	941	289	4,893
Total hardwoods	215,635	22,168	19,676	173,791
All species	267,703	29,641	30,530	207,531

Numbers in rows and columns may not sum to totals due to rounding.